THE BEGINNER'S GUIDE TO CEMETERY SLEUTHING

THE BEGINNER'S GUIDE TO CEMETERY SLEUTHING

Scavenger Hunt & Workbook

ERIN E. MOULTON

MOULTON & CASKET

For the cemetery wanderers.

May angels twine for thee,
A wreath of immortality!

—G. of New-Jersey, 1820, "To Harriet"

Contents

A Note from the Author

Dear Cemetery Sleuth,

Thank you for picking up this workbook. I hope you can find a small adventure between the pages.

Cemeteries are wonderful places to access history, genealogy, art, and stories. Each gravestone holds unique clues about the person who lies beneath it, and those clues can be a starting point to further research (and more adventure). Whether you're up for an off-the-beaten-path walk, or you're interested in diving into local history, or you're looking for more information on your ancestors, this book will be a good springboard for your journey.

I'll point out meanings behind images found on grave markers: animals, chain links, beehives, soul effigies, and more. I'll challenge you to look—and then look closer—pause, reflect, and take notes. Finally, I'll encourage you to head into archives.

So, let's go. Grab some good walking shoes, a pencil, and your workbook, and meet me at the cemetery gate. Prepare to discover something old, learn something new, and have fun doing it.

Stay curious,
Erin

How to Use This Book

Surely, reading a book is straightforward. You open it and begin to read from left to right, one page at a time. As one does. Or do you? This is a workbook. You can skip around. Here's what to know:

Part I

We start with what you'll find in a cemetery, especially on grave-stones. Each chapter has a theme. I'll offer examples and anecdotes (as I would if we were walking in a cemetery together). At the end of each chapter is a worksheet related to the chapter's theme. For example, if we just talked about occupational symbols, the end of that chapter asks you to search out occupational symbols and note them on the work-sheet. If the chapter is focused on epitaphs, the worksheet gives you space to record your favorite epitaphs, and so on.

Part II

This section brings you from the cemetery to the archives (see Appendix IV for a list of recommendations). Symbols are full of nuance. The truth is, people interpret symbols in a variety of ways. Much of the time an answer to the question *What does this symbol represent?* is *Well, that depends.* Suppose a beehive appears on a headstone. It could be a sign of a productive life or a deceased beekeeper or the Daughters of Rebekah. Context clarifies symbols, which is why the second half of this book is dedicated to research. We can gather a lot when we research the person buried beneath the stone. Why make assumptions when we can seek, assess, correlate, and access information about the dead, their life story, and maybe even their beliefs? It can be as fun to dive into archives as it is to walk through a cemetery. Discovery awaits!

Back Matter

The final pages of the workbook include helpful resources and information about the research process. Two lists serve as quick alphabetized look-up guides to the symbols and abbreviations mentioned herein. They are not meant to be an exhaustive list of all cemetery symbols or abbreviations, but they'll get you started. The reading list is all about cemeteries, gravestones, and history. Finally, there are a few suggestions for digging into archives, getting involved, and then pages for personal notes and sketches.

A Note on Etiquette

A cemetery is a special place, one where serenity and quiet abide. Please follow any rules that may be posted. Remember that many cemeteries are still active, so please be respectful of services and mindful of those visiting the final resting places of loved ones.

Historic memorials—many well over 100 and 200 years old—may be fragile. As a general rule, never sit, walk, or lean on monuments as they may break or topple over. Unless you're properly trained, I'd also discourage any cleaning or grave rubbing, which can cause unintentional damage to stones. There are often ways to be involved with cemetery work and preservation projects at the local level. See Chapter Thirteen for ideas to get started.

PART I

One

DEPICTIONS OF ANIMALS AND PLANTS

Donahue Memorial, Forest Hill Cemetery,
Derry, New Hampshire.

Animals of all types are found throughout cemeteries. Some are engraved and others are three-dimensional statues. Lambs represent innocence and are typically a topper for children's gravestones, while lions adorn the resting place of a brave or honorable person, such as a soldier. Owls are emblematic of wisdom, and bees can symbolize a productive life. The butterfly, such as the one found on the Donahue stone, can indicate a journey or the transition to resurrection. Perhaps one of the most popular animals represented at a grave is our best friend, the loyal dog.

M.P.S. Saunders, Mount Auburn Cemetery, Watertown and Cambridge, Massachusetts.

The image above shows a canine guardian sitting over the grave of M.P.S.: Mary Prentiss Saunders. Mary was the only daughter of William A. Saunders and Mary Whittemore Saunders. She died of scarlet fever, at the age of six, on June 3, 1849. This loyal friend has guarded her grave ever since. As seen in the photograph, passersby often leave a stick for the faithful companion.

Harry Edward Stevens, Green Mount Cemetery, Montpelier, Vermont.

A similar monument sits in Green Mount Cemetery. This pup guards the grave of Ned, otherwise known as Harry Edward Stevens, who died young due to cancer of the stomach. The headstone reads,

NED

ONLY CHILD OF

FRED R. & HATTIE E.

STEVENS

MAY 19TH, 1875-JAN 2ND, 1849

18 BEAUTIFUL YEARS.

Notice that both dogs sit at the feet of their owners. This occasionally causes confusion as people walk by and notice only the stone and canine statue. Some come to think a dog named Ned is buried in Green Mount Cemetery when, in fact, this pup is a footstone.

Plants have been a steadfast part of cemetery iconography and funerary tradition for ages. Some, like a rose in its varying stages of bloom, can depict the length of life of the deceased, while others, like the vine, can be emblematic of life beyond death.

Emma L. Taylor, Forest Hill Cemetery, Derry, New Hampshire.

The grave of Emma L. Taylor is adorned with a tendril of ivy. Winding things—like ivy and snakes—tend to demonstrate an ability to extend into eternity. Simply put, they indicate immortality or everlasting life. Emma Taylor and her sister Harriet founded the first public library in Derry, which is aptly named the Taylor Library. The ivy seems especially fitting since her legacy extends to the present day.

Mary J. Barker, Woodland Cemetery, Bethel, Maine.

This unique headstone sits above Mary J. Barker. Both the tree stump and the rose are meaningful. The tree stump indicates a life cut short and the rose indicates beauty. This was a young girl of just 16 years of age. Her life was cut mid bloom, so it is a fitting memorial.

Joseph Wilson, Cemetery on the Plains, Windham, New Hampshire.

The headstone of young Joseph Wilson shows off two plants. At the top, we see the weeping willow. While some believe this to be a sign of mourning, it has also been interpreted as a symbol of everlasting life/immortality. Below the willow, we see three stylized lilies. A lily is a symbol of innocence or purity. The motif on the upper part of the stone seems to tell a resurrection story: lilies (innocent life), stairs (ascension), and willow (immortality).

ANIMALS AND PLANTS

ANIMALS

- [ ] Bee: a productive life
- [ ] Bird: flight of the soul
- [ ] Butterfly: metamorphosis, here or after death
- [ ] Dog: guardian, loyalty, and love
- [ ] Lamb: innocence (often topping children's graves)
- [ ] Lion: courage, power, honor
- [ ] Owl: wisdom
- [ ] Rooster: new dawn in the afterlife, resurrection
- [ ] Snake: eternal life
- [ ] Other: ____

PLANTS

- [ ] Corn: full life, maturity, harvest
- [ ] Flowers (in general): beauty
- [ ] Ivy: friendship, life after death
- [ ] Lily or lily of the valley: innocence, purity
- [ ] Rose: beauty (a rosebud shows a life ended before bloom)
- [ ] Tree stump: life cut short
- [ ] Vine: faithfulness, remembrance
- [ ] Weeping willow: mourning and immortality
- [ ] Wreath: everlasting life
- [ ] Other: ____

Two

OCCUPATIONAL SYMBOLS

Daniel J. Day, Forest Hill Cemetery, Derry,
New Hampshire

Occupational symbols can be a fascinating jumping off point for further research. Some occupational symbols are agricultural, such as the one above. A shock of wheat, a hoe, and a stalk of corn can all be indicative of a farmer. Sometimes, though, the shock of corn or wheat can mean divine harvest (death), so it's always a great idea to do research on the deceased to gather context. Daniel J. Day was both a reverend and a farmer, so this symbol fits him quite well. Other common occupational symbols might include trees for the logger, a loom for the weaver, an anchor for the mariner or sailor, the scales of justice for a judge or lawyer, and so on.

Jibran Yusuf Skeirik, United Lebanese Cemetery/Syrian Cemetery, Andover, Massachusetts.

Rod of Asclepius, symbol of the god of healing.

In the United Lebanese Cemetery lie the remains of Jibran Yusuf Skeirik. At the turn of the 20th century, Jibran came to America from Qob Elias, Lebanon, and settled in Lawrence. He began his young working career as a grocer and then went to school to become a doctor. The symbol on his grave shows us that he became a physician. This symbol is called caduceus (kuh DOO see uhs), which is associated with Hermes, the messenger between the world of the living and the world of the divine in Greek mythology. A symbol that looks very similar to a caduceus is the rod of Asclepius (uh SKLEE pee uhs) (left). Many identify this as the only true medical symbol because Asclepius was the Greco-Roman god of healing. It's possible that the caduceus became a medical symbol because of Hermes's tie to alchemy or his travel between worlds; however, it's also likely that people have mistaken the caduceus symbol for the rod of Asclepius for so long, it has become the norm. Perhaps with its more elaborate look, it was better for marketing. What do you think? For our purposes, either symbol can indicate a doctor, nurse, or other professional in the field of medicine.

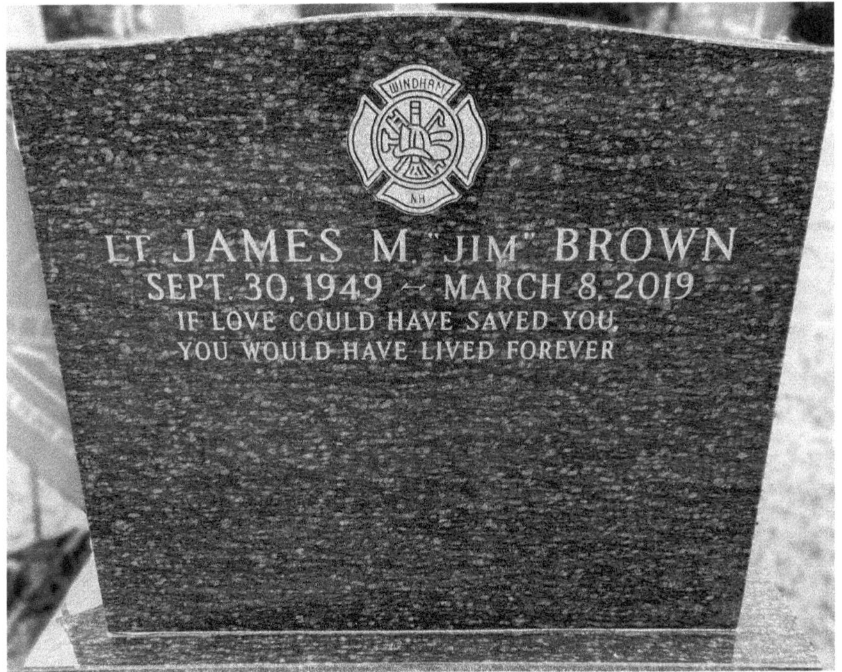

Lt. James M. "Jim" Brown with firefighter insignia, Cemetery on the Plains, Windham, New Hampshire.

Most people can recognize the occupational symbol at the top of Lt. Jim Brown's stone in an instant. He was a fireman of course. We see a firefighter hat, ladder, and ax pressed against a Maltese cross. This cross is also known as the Cross of Promise and is believed to have been the symbol of the knights of Malta. Each segment of the cross has two points, indicating the eight qualities of a knight: 1) loyalty, 2) piety, 3) generosity, 4) courage, 5) honor and glory, 6) contempt of death, 7) helpfulness, and 8) reverence for the church. While not all firefighters are religious, one can see why the symbol of ancient knights appeals to firefighters. They save people. Jim was a 48-year veteran of the

Windham fire department, setting a record for continuous service in a single department. He also regularly organized charitable fundraisers to fight muscular dystrophy. Loyalty, generosity, courage, helpfulness: That tracks!

Florence B. Garland, Cemetery on the Plains, Windham, New Hampshire.

A book doesn't always represent a writer, but in this case it surely does. The literary headstone of Florence B. Garland is the perfect monument for a teacher and scribe. The local paper, the *Windham News*, notes that Florence was a fine poet who could spin a reputable verse on a whim. The back "cover" of the monument proves the point, showcasing a few of her choice lines:

I LIKE, ON A SUMMER EVENING,
   WHEN THE LONG DAY'S WORK IS DONE
TO SIT ON THE SIDE PIAZZA
   AND WATCH AS THE SETTING SUN
THROWS RAYS OF RADIANT GLORY
   OVER SOFT PILED CLOUDS SO WHITE . . .

Fred R. Smith, Irasville Cemetery, Waitsfield, Vermont.

Many occupational symbols are self-evident, such as this fiddle engraved on the stone of Fred R. Smith. Clearly, the fiddle was an important part of Fred's life, but was he a musician, a teacher of music, or something else? A symbol and a question offer an avenue of research. If we follow that avenue, we run square into a headline in the local newspaper. On August 15, 1970, the *Times Argus* ran the article "Bill Royer and Fred Smith Fiddle to Top Spots in Chelsea Contest." He must have been good.

Wallace and Edna (Ferris) Howe, Irasville Cemetery, Waitsfield, Vermont.

This tree resides over the resting place of Wallace and Edna (Ferris) Howe. Rather than depicting a life cut short, like many tree stumps, this one is indicative of the lumber industry. How do we know this? Context! Research reveals that for a long time, the Howes found success in lumber. Wallace was part owner of the Tracy and Howe Lumber Co.

Interestingly, on January 31, 1907, the *Saint Albans Weekly Messenger* reported that a baby had been left on Edna and Wallace's doorstep in a dress suitcase with a tag on it marked "Tracy and Howe." Perhaps the person leaving the baby knew he would be well provided for.

Edna and Wallace adopted a total of three children before Edna passed away in 1907 at the age of 32. Wallace later married Hattie Kilpatrick and went into real estate, passing away in 1947. Despite the length of time between their deaths (40 years), this memorial is symbolic of the importance of Wallace and Edna's early enterprise and life together.

OCCUPATIONAL SYMBOLS

- [ ] Anchor: mariner or sailor
- [ ] Book: scholar, writer, librarian, teacher
- [ ] Caduceus or rod of Asclepius: doctor, nurse, medical work
- [ ] Chisel and mallet: craftsman - leather, stone, or wood
- [ ] Engine or gears: engineer
- [ ] Hoe / shock of wheat / plow: farmer
- [ ] Maltese cross: firefighter
- [ ] Mortar and pestle: apothecary or pharmacist
- [ ] Musical notes or musical instrument: musician
- [ ] Scales of justice: lawyer or judge
- [ ] Tree: lumberer, forester, woodcrafter

The occupational symbols in your local cemetery can reveal information about the local economy and industry of the past. What other occupations or tools of the trade can you find?

____

____

____

____

____

____

____

____

____

Three

DEATH'S-HEADS AND SOUL EFFIGIES

Margaret Park, winged death's-head, Forest Hill Cemetery, Derry, New Hampshire.

Sometimes you will find yourself staring at a headstone, and the headstone is staring back. Especially in graveyards from the Colonial times, you might come across some intriguing faces. These are death's-heads, winged death's-heads, and soul effigies. Let's take a look.

William Greig, death's-head, Forest Hill Cemetery, Derry, New Hampshire.

Death's-heads were carved on headstones across New England (and beyond) in the 17th and 18th centuries. The death's-head is typically a skull or a skull and crossbones and has been interpreted by many to indicate a place of mortal remains. This one adorns the headstone of William Greig, a first settler of Nutfield, who passed away in 1752.

Abial Cross, winged death's-head, Salem Center Burying Ground, Salem, New Hampshire.

Winged death's-heads look exactly as they sound. They are depicted as a skull with wings on either side. Most often, this has been interpreted as "mortal remains" and "ascent of the soul." This winged death's-head sits over the resting place of Abial Cross, who died at the age of 35 in 1778.

William Graham, soul effigy, Chester Village Cemetery, Chester, New Hampshire.

Soul effigies are lifelike faces with wings on either side. Some suggest that they are a close representation of the deceased; however, many of the faces look extremely similar. Also, let's think about the stone carvers. They would have had to work off a painting, a corpse, or personal memory to achieve a likeness. What a burdensome process! That's not to say there isn't a hand carved portrait of your ancestor out there. It's just more rare than you might think. In any case, the meaning of these soul effigies is similar to the winged death's-head (mortal remains and ascent of the soul). This soul effigy resides above William Graham's resting place in the Chester Village Cemetery. He passed away in 1789.

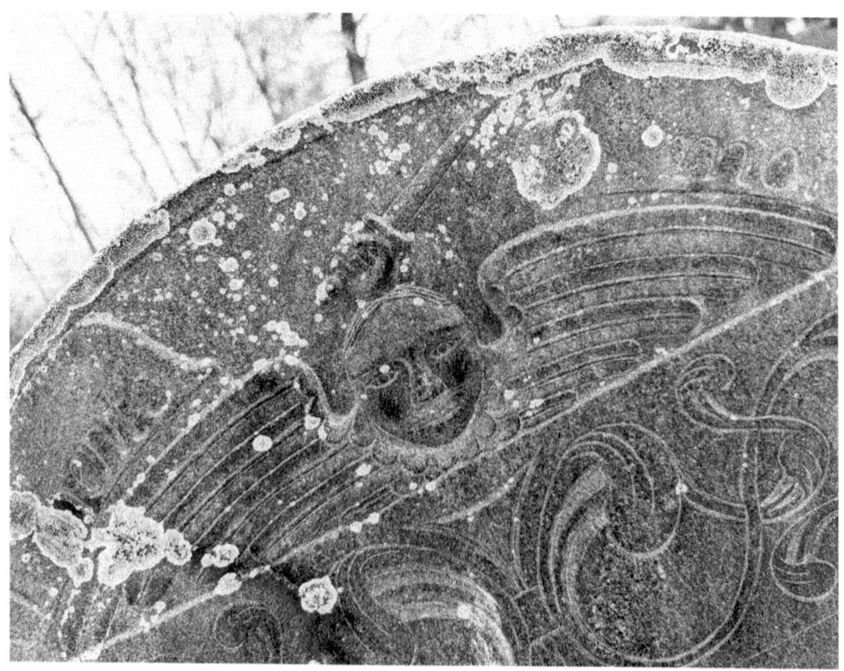

Colonel Robert Moor, soul effigy with dagger, Forest Hill Cemetery, Derry, New Hampshire.

Even if the faces of soul effigies don't represent the deceased, exactly, many have a unique detail that is particular to them. The soul effigy that sits over the resting place of Colonel Robert Moor sports a hand holding a dagger. Colonel Moor died on October 25, 1778. This image seems to indicate the colonel's fighting spirit. Perhaps he even went down in battle. It's a thought that sparks further research.

DEATH'S-HEADS

What death's-heads do you see in the cemetery?
Can you locate names and dates?

NAME OF DECEASED	DATE OF BIRTH	DATE OF DEATH	OTHER NOTES

WINGED DEATH'S-HEADS

What winged death's-heads do you see in the cemetery?
Can you locate names and dates?

NAME OF DECEASED	DATE OF BIRTH	DATE OF DEATH	OTHER NOTES

SOUL EFFIGIES

What soul effigies can you find in the cemetery?
Take a close look to see if they have any unique features.
What do they tell you about the departed?

NAME OF DECEASED	DATE OF BIRTH AND DEATH	UNIQUE FEATURE	OTHER NOTES

Four

VETERANS MARKERS

US Veteran marker, Cemetery on the Plains,
Windham, New Hampshire.

According to the US Department of Veterans Affairs (VA), they will furnish a headstone or marker for the grave of any deceased *eligible* veteran in any cemetery around the world, regardless of their date of death. These headstones are all around you and can give you valuable clues about the veteran's service. Because these stones are government issued, there is consistency in terms of design and inscriptions. The parameters have changed over time, beginning with the most basic design prior to the Civil War to a more centralized one during the Civil War. From then until present day, the government-issued headstones have evolved even more. Let me show you what I mean.

Robt. B. Oakes, Company E, 1st Massachusetts Heavy Artillery Regiment, Cemetery on the Plains, Windham, New Hampshire.

Civil War and Spanish-American War headstones furnished by the VA can be identified as a simple granite or marble upright with a rounded top with raised lettering on an indented shield. These typically include a name, company, and regiment. In this case (above), we have ROBT. B. OAKES, with the shorthand CO. E 1 MASS. H.A. This indicates that Robert was part of Company E of the 1st Massachusetts Heavy Artillery Regiment of the Union Army during the Civil War. Just a few letters and some curiosity can give you a pathway into research. Where was Company E stationed? What does Heavy Artillery mean? What action did Robert see?

From World War I to present day, the stones include more information such as the soldier's name, military branch, rank abbreviation, and even emblem of belief. These details can give valuable context and a jumping-off point for research.

James C. Greenhalgh, Forest Hill Cemetery, Derry, New Hampshire.

The marker of James C. Greenhalgh includes a wheel, revealing that he was Buddhist. The rank abbreviation and branch, HT2 US NAVY, tells us he was a Hull Maintenance Technician Petty Officer 2nd Class for the US Navy.

Donald Tower Hills, Forest Hill Cemetery, Derry, New Hampshire.

While Donald Tower Hills's marker is slightly overgrown, we can still gather valuable information. His emblem of belief is the Latin cross, denoting Christianity. He served in the US Army and Navy. He served during the Korean War. His navy rank abbreviation, GMG3, indicates he was a Gunner's Mate Petty Officer 3rd Class.

Morton C. Pearlman, Cemetery on the Plains, Windham, New Hampshire.

The headstone of Morton C. Pearlman has many hints for the researcher. First, the rank abbreviation, RMN3 US NAVY indicates he was Radioman (Navigation) Petty Officer 3rd Class for the US Navy.

We can see he served during the Korean War. His emblem of belief at the center of the stone is the Star of David, indicating that he was Jewish. We also see he was a husband, father, and grandfather. We have under 100 characters on this stone, but so many places to begin research on his life, career, and even family.

It can be a lot of fun and a big project to decipher these grave markers. Especially for those of us with no military background, this is an unknown world with its own language. You know what I think? I think it's more important to find and utilize a good resource than it is to try to remember everything. We can rely on resources at the National Cemetery Association, Department of Veterans Affairs, to help us understand the emblems of belief and rank abbreviations.

- Emblems of Belief: https://www.cem.va.gov/hmm/emblems.asp

- Inscription Abbreviations: https://www.cem.va.gov/hmm /inscriptions.asp#Abbreviations

It's time to hit the cemetery and identify some veterans.

VETERANS MARKERS
CIVIL WAR AND SPANISH-AMERICAN WAR

Seek out veterans markers. Find and record the name of the veteran, company, and regiment of each.

NAME OF VETERAN	COMPANY	REGIMENT	OTHER NOTES

VETERANS MARKERS
WWI TO PRESENT DAY

Seek out veterans markers. Find and record the emblem of belief, rank abbreviation, and service branch of each.

NAME OF VETERAN	EMBLEM OF BELIEF	RANK ABBREVIATION AND SERVICE BRANCH	OTHER NOTES

Five

HALLMARKS OF ORGANIZATIONS, CLUBS, AND SECRET SOCIETIES

Philip Godfrid Kast, Freemason, Forest Hill
Cemetery, Derry, New Hampshire.

There are many symbols associated with clubs, fraternal organizations, and so-called secret societies. Once you know the basic symbols, you'll begin to see these everywhere. Let's unpack some before your imagination starts to conjure up a local, symbol-based thriller that rivals *The Da Vinci Code*. Then again, if you do write that, I'm here for it.

Freemasons: compass and square with G at center.

Freemasons: One of the most commonly used symbols of the Freemasons is the one above. This is the compass and the square with a *G* at the center. The symbol indicates one of the most important aspects of Freemasonry, geometry. It's a nod to divine architecture, the stonemasons of centuries past who began the order, and the idea that Masonry *builds* better men. While you may see this symbol most, Freemasons love symbolism and there are many more Masonic symbols to discover at the end of this chapter.

Order of the Eastern Star: five-pointed star with the initials OES.

Order of the Eastern Star: The Order of the Eastern Star is a branch of Masonry that began as the female auxiliary. A man named Rob Morris established this order in Mississippi in the 1850s in order to bring women into Masonry who were already related by blood or marriage to a Mason. This was called *Adoptive Masonry,* which was a practice abroad, much earlier than the inception of the order in the US. Their most common symbol is the five-pointed star accompanied by the initials *OES.* In more complicated variations of the symbol, the details of each part of the star includes iconography associated with the biblical heroines: Adah, Ruth, Esther, Martha, and Electa.

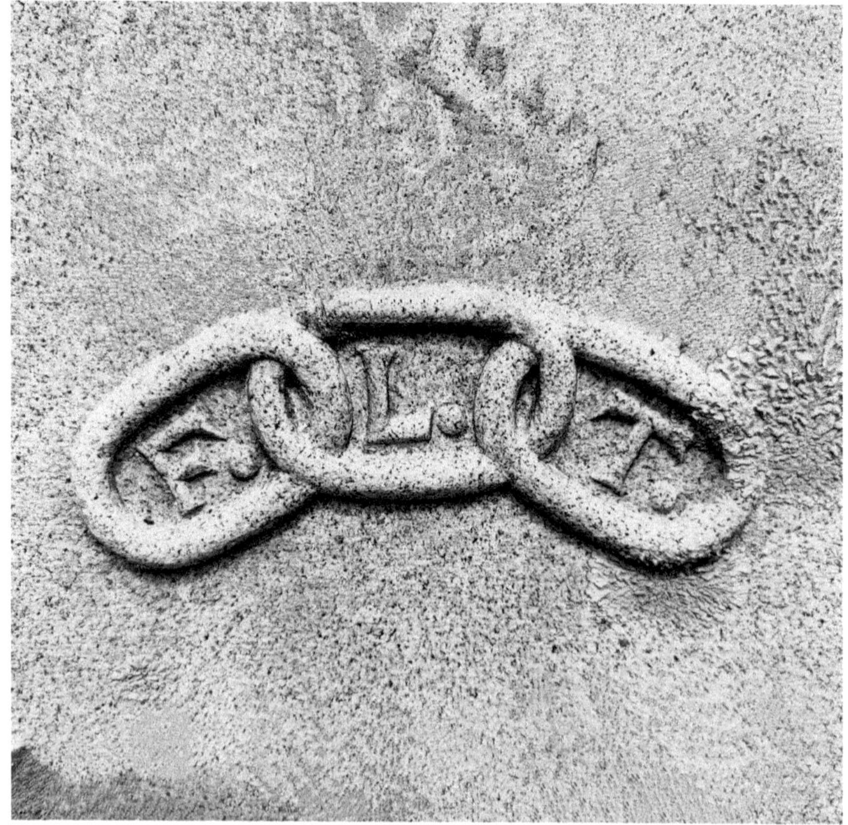

Independent Order of the Oddfellows: three links with the initials FLT.

Independent Order of the Oddfellows: When the Oddfellows were founded is hard to say; some date it back to medieval trade guilds. Think of it like a workman's networking group. Imagine you're a blacksmith who lives in village A and you have to move to village B. If you have no friends or associates in village B, it could be complicated to find work. If you're an Oddfellow, you show up at the Village B lodge, you meet your brethren, and you are welcomed in. The connections begin. The Oddfellows have many symbols, but the three links is their most recognized. Within the links, you can see the abbreviation *FLT*. That stands for their three most important teachings, the tenets that bind them: friendship, love, and truth.

Daughters of Rebekah: crescent moon, seven stars, dove, lily, beehive, and the letter R.

Daughters of Rebekah (also known as the Rebekahs or the International Order of Rebekahs Assemblies) is a branch of the Oddfellows, which began as the female auxiliary. The Rebekahs was established in 1851. Typically, their emblem includes the beehive, representing the busy members of the lodge; the lily for purity; the dove for peace; and the moon and stars, indicating the good life guided by the divine. In other iterations, you can also see three links around the *R*, which clearly indicate the association with the Oddfellows.

Knights of Columbus: Maltese cross with ax, anchor, sword, and the initials K of C.

Knights of Columbus: The Knights of Columbus was founded in 1882 by Father Michael J. McGivney as a charitable foundation. The insignia has a shield against a Maltese cross. It also includes an ax, sword, and anchor and usually the initials for the foundation. The shield and cross are meant to represent the Catholic spirit. The anchor symbolizes the patron of the order (Christopher Columbus). The ax represents fraternal bond, and the sword represents honor.

Knights of Pythias: armor, shield, battle axes, and swords with the initials FBC.

Knights of Pythias: This organization was established in 1864. Founded by Justus Rathbone, it was the first fraternal organization to be chartered under an act of the US Congress. If you see shields, battle-axes, and armor with the initials *K of P* or *FBC*, you're looking at a member of the Knights of Pythias. Of course, *K of P* is the abbreviation for the order, while *FBC* stands for their three main tenets: friendship, benevolence, and charity.

Pythian Sisters: sword, wand, and crown with the initials PS and/or PLEF.

Pythian Sisters: The Pythian Sisters were established in 1888. Some credit the founding of the Pythian Sisters to a man named Joseph Addison Hill and others point toward New Hampshire's Mrs. A. A. Young. The symbol for the Pythian Sisters typically includes a wand, a sword, and a crown, often in front of a Maltese cross. The *PS* on either side of the symbol indicates the name of the sisterhood, while *PLEF* stands for purity, love, equality, and fidelity.

Fraternal Order of the Eagles: an eagle with a shield holding a serpent and the initials FOE.

Fraternal Order of the Eagles: I bet you weren't going to guess that this organization had its roots in theater. The story goes that in 1898 six competing theater owners came together to discuss a looming musicians' strike. Soon, they had reconciled and agreed to band together to form a club that was originally called the Order of Good Things. They had large growth in the early days due to the popularity of traveling theater troupes. Their mission evolved over time, and today it is "to unite fraternally in the spirit of liberty, truth, justice, and equality, to make human life more desirable by lessening its ills and promoting peace, prosperity, gladness and hope." Their insignia includes an eagle holding a serpent. Their lodges are called Aeries, so if you see an eagle, the letters *FOE*, or any indication of Aerie, you have come across a member of the Fraternal Order of the Eagles.

The National Grange: sheaf of wheat with the initials P and H.

The National Grange: This organization focuses on family, community well-being, and agriculture. It was founded in 1867 by Oliver Hudson Kelley and others to promote and advocate for the economic requirements of farmers. The Grange included women in its elected offices from the early days. When Oliver was laying out his plan for the organization of farmers, he went to visit his niece, Caroline Arabella Hall, in Boston and asked for her opinion. She gave enthusiastic feedback and suggested women have full membership in the organization. From then on, she was an integral part of the founding of the Grange. Caroline served as first Ceres (think master of ceremonies for rituals), Worthy Lady Assistant Steward, and she compiled the first songbook. The Grange symbol is identified by a sheaf of wheat with the initials *P* and *H* on either side. *P* and *H* stand for "Patrons of Husbandry."

Girl Scouts: eagle with shield, olive branch, and quiver of arrows pressed against trefoil with the initials GS.

Girl Scouts of the USA: The Girl Scouts was established in 1912 by Juliette Gordon Low (Daisy) to encourage girls' unique strengths and passions. If you look closely at the insignia, you can identify an eagle, a shield, an olive branch, and a quiver of arrows. The image is pressed against the trefoil (defined as a plant with three-lobed leaves), which represents the three-fold promise of the Girl Scouts, which are to 1) do duty to God and country; 2) help other people at all times; 3) obey the Scout laws. We especially see this symbol if the deceased was a lifelong scout or troop leader.

Boy Scouts: eagle with shield and American flag against a fleur-de-lis.

Boy Scouts of America: The Boy Scouts was established in 1910 by W. D. Boyce. The story goes that Boyce had been lost in London and was guided to his destination by a random boy. The boy refused a tip and explained that it was his duty as a member of the Boy Scouts Association (established in Britain in 1908). Boyce modeled the Boy Scouts of America after its British counterpart. The Boy Scouts logo is an eagle with a shield and an American flag. The image is pressed against a fleur-de-lis, which represents the compass and serves as a reminder to the scout to head in the right direction. The stars, left and right, represent truth and knowledge. The eagle with shield represents freedom and the readiness to defend freedom. This symbol can be seen on headstones of longtime scouts or, as in this case, can signal a cemetery-based Scout project. An Eagle Scout from Troop 263 restored the veterans walkway and flagpole area in the Cemetery on the Plains in Windham, New Hampshire.

Daughters of the American Revolution: spinning wheel and distaff.

Daughters of the American Revolution: The DAR was established in 1890 by Mary Smith Lockwood, Eugenia Washington, Ellen Hardin Walworth, and Mary Desha. The DAR is a lineage-based service organization made up of women who are direct descendants of a patriot of the American Revolution or someone who had a direct and established involvement with American Independence. Their insignia consists of a spinning wheel and a distaff (a short rod used for holding wool or flax while spinning).

Sons of the American Revolution: Cross of St. Louis and laurel wreath.

Sons of the American Revolution: The SAR was established in 1889, largely led by William Osborn McDowell. The SAR is a lineage-based service organization composed of men who are direct descendants of a patriot who served in the American Revolution. The insignia includes the Cross of St. Louis and the laurel wreath and typically includes the initials *SAR*.

More Masonic Symbols

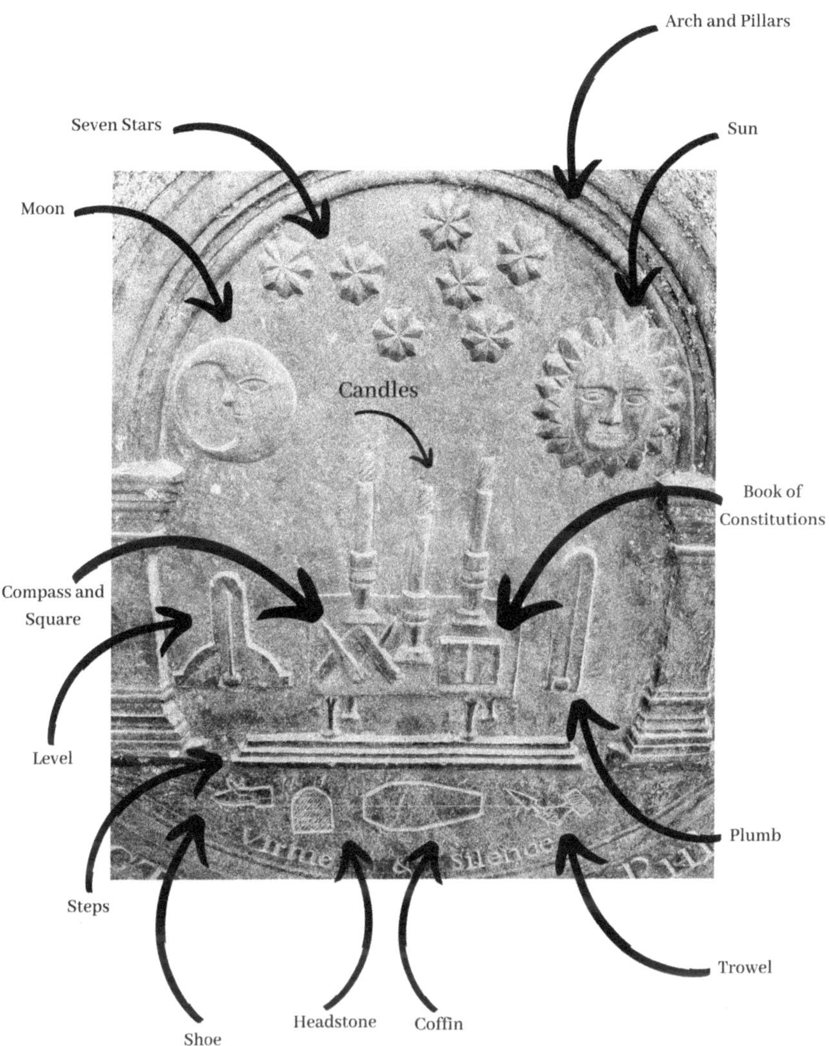

Philip Godfrid Kast, Masonic symbols, Forest Hill Cemetery, Derry, New Hampshire.

Philip Godfrid Kast's stone was posthumously erected by fellow Masons. It gives us a good idea of Philip's importance in the order as nearly every symbol on the stone is meaningful. Even for non-Masons, understanding the symbology is possible. In this case, we can rely on

An Encyclopedia of Freemasonry and Its Kindred Sciences: Comprising the Whole Range of Arts, Sciences and Literature as Connected with the Institution (Vols. 1 and 2) by Albert Gallatin Mackey.

Arch and Pillars: The arch and pillars are a nod to those of Solomon's Temple. Solomon is considered the blueprint, the original Mason, and many facets of the later lodges mimicked those of his temple. Another interpretation may be that the arch is emblematic of heaven or the Holy Royal Arch, the higher degree of Masonry. The pillars could indicate two elements essential to the role of the higher Mason: wisdom and strength.

Book of Constitutions: The open book symbolizes the guidebook for the Masons, the *Book of Constitutions*. Sometimes this is seen with Tyler's Sword, which reminds the Mason to guard against enemies of Masonry.

Candles: The image of three candles mimics the three in a Masonic lodge, which represent the sun, the moon, and the Master Mason. The sun rules the day; the moon rules the night; and the Master Mason rules the lodge.

Coffin: While not unique to the Masons, a coffin is commonly used as an emblem of mortal remains.

Compass and Square: The compass and square indicate the most important branch of science to the Masons: geometry. It's a nod to the divine architect and a reminder to stay curious, observe the makings of the universe, and be methodical.

Headstone: Similar to the coffin, a headstone is emblematic of mortal remains/burial.

Level: This tool is used by stonemasons to make sure a line is horizontal. The symbol reminds Masons to remember the equality of man and to walk, steadfastly, "the level of time."

Moon: The moon appears in Masonic symbolism as the balance to the sun, a guide in the night.

Plumb: A plumb is an instrument used to make sure that a building is perfectly vertical. The symbol is a reminder to Masons to be upright in their endeavors. In other words, the Mason should be moral, equitable, and honest.

Seven Stars: Seven is a sacred number to Masons and harkens back to the seven liberal arts and sciences that were the foundation of Masonry, the trivium and quadrivium, the sum of all knowledge. The trivium includes grammar, rhetoric, and logic. The quadrivium includes arithmetic, geometry, harmony, and astronomy. Notice that the stars on the stone are grouped into clusters of three and four.

Shoe: The shoe indicates an offering and seals a pact. In the first degree, the giving of the shoe indicates the commitment to the lodge. In the case of this particular headstone, it may represent the practice of removing one's shoes upon entering a house of God.

Steps: Three steps indicate the three seasons of a Mason's life: youth, manhood, and age.

Sun: The sun is a symbol of intellectual light that Masons should always seek.

Trowel: This is the working tool of the Master Mason. The implement is used to spread the cement that will hold the entire building together, and it is a reminder that the Masons' work is to spread affection and kindness (brotherly love).

Want even more Masonic symbols? Let's take a moment to look closer at the Howe memorial in Irasville Cemetery in Waitsfield, Vermont (see p. 14). The plot reveals that the Howes were interested in more than lumber. At the end of Edna's and Wallace's headstones, which look like felled trees, we can see other symbols affiliated with the Masons.

Wallace Howe

Edna (Ferris) Howe

Wallace and Edna (Ferris) Howe, Masonic and Order of the Eastern Star symbols, Irasville Cemetery, Waitsfield, Vermont.

Wallace Howe's stone shows a two-headed eagle with a triangle and the number 32 at center. This symbolizes the Ancient and Accepted Scottish Rite of Freemasonry. The triangle represents the 32nd degree of the Scottish Rite.

Edna (Ferris) Howe's stone shows off the five-pointed star associated with the Order of the Eastern Star. Each point alternates with the letters *FATAL*. This looks grim, but according to the *Ritual of the Order of the Eastern Star: A Book of Instruction for the Organization, Government and Ceremonies of the Chapters of the Order in Every Department* by Robert Macoy, it simply means "Fairest Among Thousands, Altogether Lovely."

More Symbols of the Independent Order of the Oddfellows

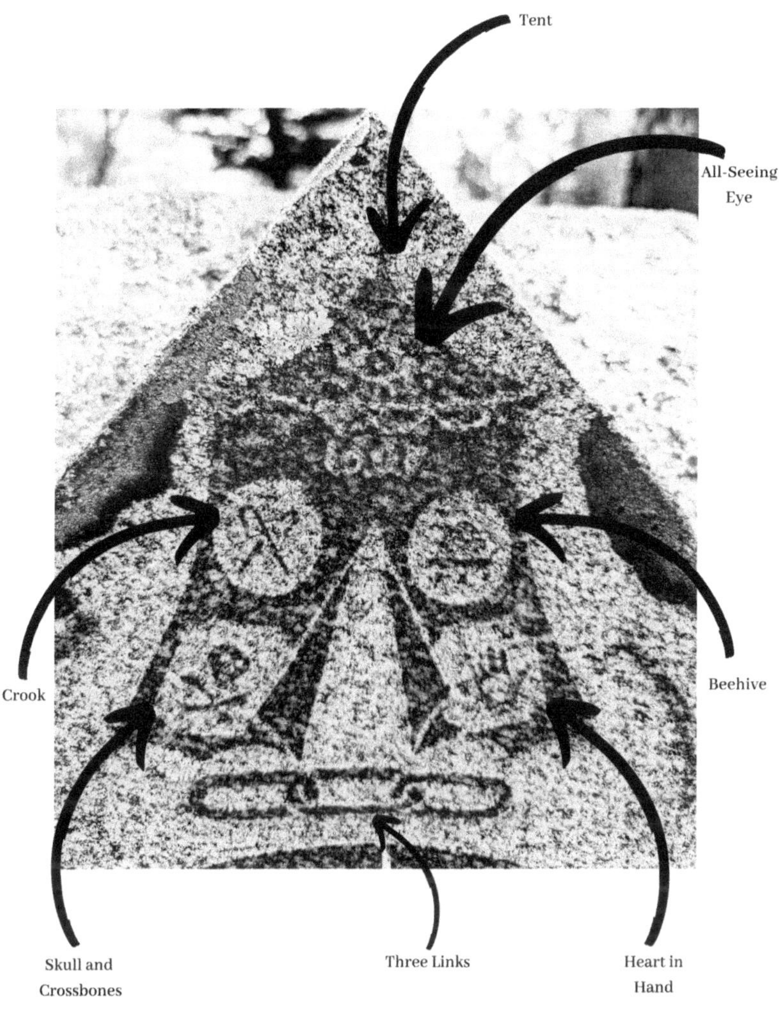

T. R. and Louisa Robie, IOOF symbols, Forest Hill Cemetery, Derry, New Hampshire.

The Masons aren't the only ones with a wide variety of symbols. The weather worn headstone over the resting place of T.R. (Tappan) Robie includes several symbols associated with the Independent Order of the Oddfellows. The text *Odd-Fellows Improved Manual* by Reverend A. B. Grosh helps us navigate the meaning of some of these emblems.

All-Seeing Eye (omniscience) Essentially, this is God's eye and a reminder to the Oddfellow that God is watching his every word and deed. It reminds the Oddfellow to have integrity.

Beehive (industry) To the Oddfellow, the beehive is a reminder of the benefits of working together. Not only is it important to aid the others in the hive (fellow man) but also remember the role one plays in the hive. Each industrious bee has a job and if they toil together, they will reap the benefits in due time.

Crook (guidance and protection) The crook is the shepherd's tool. It is emblematic of the wisdom of the Great Shepherd and reminds the Oddfellow to be a good leader to his own flock.

Heart in Hand (sincerity) This emblem is like wearing "one's heart on one's sleeve." In other words, be authentic in actions. The Oddfellow should be heart forward in word and deed and remember to give openly both in feeling and in charity.

Skull and Crossbones (mortality) This symbol reminds the Oddfellow of their own mortality, but it also serves as a reminder to honor the brothers who have already gone by and to put them to rest with proper attention and ritual. It is a warning, too, to throw off earthly vanity and act in a Godly way.

Tent (hospitality) This emblem, to the Oddfellow, is a bit like saying "my door is always open." It is an invitation to enter and a reminder to the members that they were welcomed into the tent when they were in need.

Three Links (friendship, love, and truth) The three links represent the encircling chain that binds the Oddfellows in sympathy and in one another's well-being. It reminds the Oddfellow that a good life is based upon the practice of friendship, love, and truth.

HALLMARKS OF ORGANIZATIONS, CLUBS, AND SECRET SOCIETIES

Motifs and abbreviations often indicate a group or club.
Do you find members of any of the following?

- ☐ Boy Scouts of America: eagle with shield and American flag, pressed against a fleur-de-lis
- ☐ Daughters of Rebekah: dove, beehive, lily, and crescent moon
- ☐ Fraternal Order of the Eagles: eagle and serpent with the initials *FO.*
- ☐ Freemasons: compass and square with letter *G*
- ☐ Girl Scouts of the USA: eagle, shield, olive branch, quiver of arrows, and trefoil
- ☐ National Grange: sheaf of wheat with initials *P* and *H*
- ☐ Independent Order of the Oddfellows: three chain links with initials *FLT* or *IOOF*
- ☐ Knights of Columbus: shield, ax, anchor, and sword with initials *K* o
- ☐ Knights of Pythias: armor with initials *K* of *P* or *FBC*
- ☐ Order of the Eastern Star: five-pointed star with initials *OES*
- ☐ Pythian Sisters: wand, sword, and crown with initials *PS* and/or *PLE*

BONUS MASONIC AND IOOF SYMBOLS

- ☐ Level or plumb
- ☐ Seven stars
- ☐ Trowel
- ☐ Heart in hand
- ☐ Shepherd's crook
- ☐ Beehive
- ☐ Five-pointed star with initials *FATAL*

OTHER COMMON SYMBOLS

Hannah and Lucinda Hill, Cemetery on the
Plains, Windham, New Hampshire.

There certainly are many symbols to see in a cemetery—so many it can be difficult to keep track. The following pages include some of the other common symbols you can look for: hands, urns, books, angels, and more.

Margaret Head, handshake, Head Cemetery, Hooksett, New Hampshire.

Hands can indicate God, spirituality, or the divine realm. They are seen in varying forms throughout the cemetery. A handshake depicts a soul's welcome into heaven. Though, if the sleeve cuffs are different, as seen above, the clasp may be indicating a parting of ways, particularly between a couple. It can show a strong bond, a fond farewell.

Jacob Harris, finger pointing up, Cemetery on the Plains, Windham, New Hampshire.

A finger pointing up indicates a soul's journey to heaven. Contrary to popular belief, a finger pointing down does not mean a soul going to hell. Rather, it symbolizes God's hand reaching down to bring a soul to heaven.

Charles Davidson, urn with flame and shroud, Cemetery on the
Plains, Windham, New Hampshire.

Urns are another common symbol we see in cemeteries. Sometimes
they are alone, sometimes they are aflame, and at other times they
include a drape or shroud. The urn by itself depicts mortal remains.
The flame symbolizes undying friendship. The shroud or drape can
symbolize the veil between worlds, God's protection, or mourning.

Sarah D. Morrison, urn and weeping willow motif, Forest Hill
Cemetery, Derry, New Hampshire.

The weeping willow and urn motif was popular in the 1800s. The urn represents mortal remains. The weeping willow represents immortality. The stairs that the urns and willow rest on show ascension. This motif seems to tell the story of life after death, a belief in life in a heavenly realm.

Foster Dana, Book of Life, Warren Village Cemetery, Warren, Vermont.

We've seen an example of a book with poetic verse on it in conjunction with a writer/educator but, more often than not, when you see a book in the cemetery it is meant to depict the Book of Life or the Bible.

COMMON SYMBOLS

☐ Book or book and hand: Bible

☐ Cross: Christianity

☐ Hand with finger pointing up: a soul to heaven

☐ Hand with finger pointing down: God reaching down to bring a soul to heaven

☐ Handshake: fond farewell, warm welcome

☐ Urn: mortal remains

☐ Urn with flame: mortal remains and undying friendship

☐ Urn with shroud: mortal remains and mourning

☐ Urn with willow: mortal remains and everlasting life

Are you up for a few more symbols and their meanings? Once you start walking through a cemetery, you're bound to see a few of these, too.

☐ Angel: heavenly messenger
☐ Coffin: mortality
☐ Harp: praise
☐ Heart: love
☐ Hourglass: time passing, sands of time
☐ Portal or door: embarking on new journey
☐ Shell: eternal life
☐ Sun rising: renewal, new beginnings

Seven

EPITAPHS

D. Gwendolyn Warmington Halvosa and William Edward K. Halvosa, "Set me as a seal upon thine heart for love is strong as death," Hope Cemetery, Barre, Vermont.

An epitaph is defined as "a phrase or form of words written in memory of a person who has died, especially as an inscription on a tombstone." Some epitaphs reflect on the life of the deceased, some ring romantic (like the one above), others tell a haunting tale.

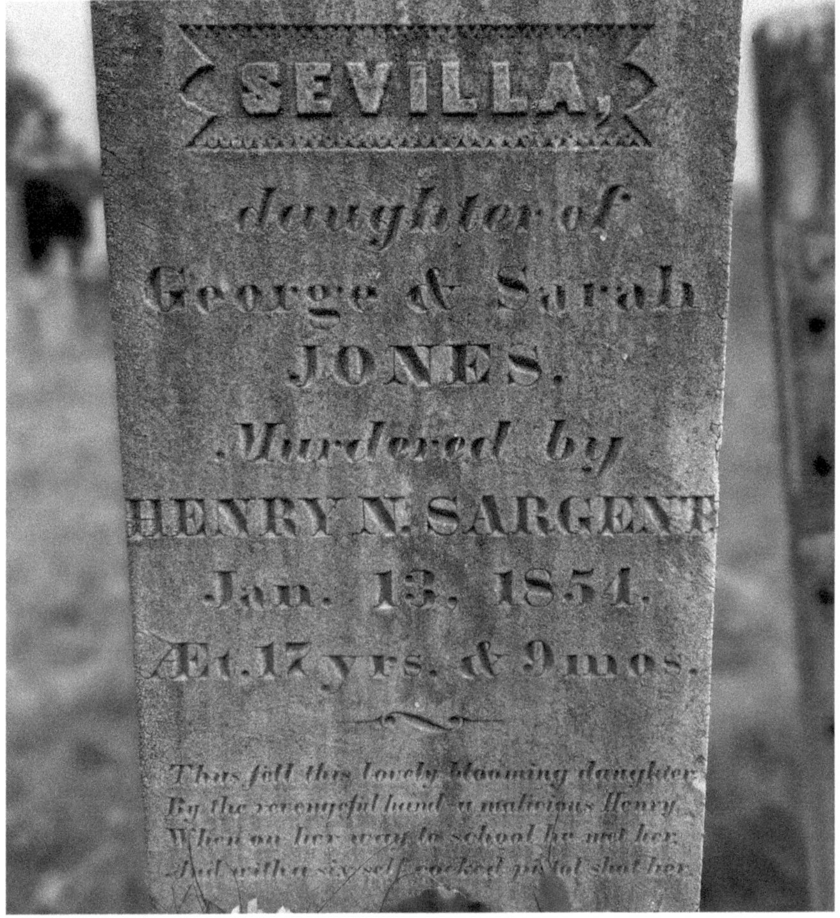

Sevilla Jones, New Boston Cemetery, New Boston, New Hampshire.

The headstone of Sevilla Jones tells the story of a tragic demise.

THUS FELL THIS LOVELY BLOOMING DAUGHTER
BY THE REVENGEFUL HAND, A MALICIOUS HENRY,
WHEN ON HER WAY TO SCHOOL HE MET HER,
AND WITH A SIX SELF COCKED PISTOL SHOT HER.

People have had strong feelings about this epitaph since it was first placed above Sevilla Jones in the 1850s. Some felt that it was unfortunate that she would have to lie under a description of her tragedy for perpetuity. Others felt that it was important that people knew her story. Either way, it's undeniably attention-grabbing. Curious people seek this stone out to this day.

Mary E. Dainty, Fairview Cemetery, New Britain, Connecticut.

During the pandemic, I went way down a family history research rabbit hole and discovered my ancestor, Mary E. Dainty, who died tragically in 1925. She was buried in Fairview Cemetery in New Britain, Connecticut, but was not given a headstone at that time. With the help of family, friends, and Instagram followers, we were able to raise the funds to get her a proper headstone. Her epitaph simply reads:

WE LOVE YOU, AND LOVE BRINGS YOU HOME.

This line from *The Boy, the Mole, the Fox and the Horse* by Charlie Mackesy was fitting for a young girl whose remains, and story, were hidden for so long.

Hannah Webster, Chester Village Cemetery, Chester, New Hampshire.

This headstone for Mrs. Hannah Webster has a classic epitaph warning passersby to reflect on their own time on this planet.

HALT PASSENGER, AS YOU GO BY;
REMEMBER MAN THAT YOU MUST DIE:
CONSIDER TIME IS RUNNING FAST,
AND DEATH WILL SURELY COME AT LAST.

Getting close to the headstone and reading an epitaph is a great practice and it can give you inspiration to think of your own. Mine? It'll probably read something like:

IT'S BEEN WEIRD.

How about yours?

EPITAPHS

Find and record your favorite epitaphs.

EPITAPHS

Find and record your favorite epitaphs.

EPITAPHS

Find and record your favorite epitaphs.

Eight

STONE CARVERS

Joslin Family Stone, Irasville Cemetery, Waitsfield, Vermont. Carved by Rock of Ages in Barre, Vermont.

Not only does the cemetery share plenty of information on the dead, but it's also a fine art gallery showcasing the product of local stone carvers and workmen. More modern stones can display a company logo, like the Rock of Ages (ROA) in the image above.

ROA was established in 1885 by George B. Milne in Barre, Vermont. In 1914, Milne and partners adopted the name Rock of Ages. They've since grown into one of North America's largest granite manufacturers. You can find these ROA stones all over Vermont and beyond. They don't always bear the logo, like the one above, but on the Joslin stone, you can clearly see their trademark. The word *Endowed* next to ROA gives us the idea that it was furnished by the company, perhaps free of charge.

As you become familiar with your cemeteries, you'll likely begin to recognize the work of local carvers. Let me show you one of my absolute favorites.

Robert Logan, Forest Hill Cemetery, Derry, New Hampshire. Carved by John Wight, the Hieroglyph Stone Carver of Londonderry.

The stone above is believed to have been carved by John Wight, otherwise known as the Coffin-Star-Heart Man, otherwise known as the Hieroglyph Stone Carver of Londonderry. He was among the first Scots-Irish settlers to arrive in Londonderry, then known as Nutfield, in 1719. He worked as a farmer and stone carver. The images on this stone are very different from the death's-heads around them. His

Coffin-Star-Heart pattern has been interpreted over the years—and in conjunction with the epitaphs—as death, heavenly realm, and a heart beating on. While John Wight didn't sign his stones, his work is quite easy to spot simply by his unique style.

Sarah D. Morrison, Forest Hill Cemetery, Derry, New Hampshire. Carved by M. Davis, Nashville (Moses Davis, Nashua).

By the early 1800s, many stone carvers would include their names at the bottom of the stone. The example above can be spotted on Sarah Morrison's stone. It says, *M. Davis, Nashville*. That's Moses Davis of Nashua, New Hampshire. He began the Davis Funeral Home in 1842, which continues business today.

Next time you're in a cemetery, be sure to glance toward the bottom of the stones to see the artists and workmen behind the designs.

STONE CARVERS

As you explore, look to the bottom of the stones and
see if you spot the name of the stone carver.
Record names you find.

1. ....
2. ....
3. ....
4. ....
5. ....
6. ....
7. ....
8. ....
9. ....
10. ....
11. ....
12. ....
13. ....
14. ....
15. ....
16. ....
17. ....
18. ....
19. ....
20. ....

Nine

A CEMETERY YEAR

Author, having a rest in Forest Hill Cemetery,
Derry, New Hampshire.

Walking in the cemetery can be an educational experience and it also gives you some great exercise. I challenge you to create a bucket list of the cemeteries you'd like to visit this year. Will you hit every cemetery in town? Will you seek out garden cemeteries? Will you explore haunted cemeteries? Will you navigate veterans cemeteries? Perhaps you will roam the oldest burial grounds. Whatever path you choose, I hope you get out there and see what you can find.

LOGBOOK

Challenge yourself to walk in a cemetery at least once a month. Log your journey and make notes about your experience.

MONTH	CEMETERY	CITY OR TOWN, STATE	NOTES
JANUARY			
FEBRUARY			
MARCH			
APRIL			
MAY			
JUNE			

LOGBOOK

Challenge yourself to walk in a cemetery at least once a month. Log your journey and make notes about your experience.

MONTH	CEMETERY	CITY OR TOWN, STATE	NOTES
JULY			
AUGUST			
SEPTEMBER			
OCTOBER			
NOVEMBER			
DECEMBER			

PART II

Ten

LOCAL STORIES

A cemetery is a perfect place to access local history. It's a local time capsule! Instead of a rusted box filled with bucket lists, archival materials, and a dilapidated Raquel Welch workout tape, a graveyard holds names, dates, and symbols. These are clues that can tell you about the lives of the locals. When you record what you see in the cemetery and then research further, you can travel to the past.

In the following pages, I'm going to share a few stories that I've put together over the years. I've done this by tracking the decedents through various archives and resources. I've spent long and happy hours squinting at vital and census records, exploring town reports, local history books, and newspapers, and delving into trade publications and deeds.

In the following pages, I'll show you the results of my labor and then send you off to do some sleuthing of your own.

Laura Perkins Darling

Laura Perkins Darling, Forest Hill Cemetery, Derry, New Hampshire.

This is the headstone of Mrs. Laura Darling. By beginning on the *Ancestry* database, then heading to online local newspaper archives, I began the search for Mrs. Darling. From there, I explored town histories, local maps, and historic deeds. Thanks to these records, I was able to track Mrs. Darling's life story and develop some context through her associations and location. Here's what I know:

Mrs. Darling was born Laura Perkins in 1853. Her father, Spencer Perkins, was a "Cattle Slaughterer," her mother, Martha (Williams) Perkins, kept house. They lived in Old Town, Maine, defined by its Abenaki history and roaring Penobscot River. By the age of 17, Laura had married 28-year-old James P. Darling. James was a veteran of the Civil War and had fought with the 5th New Hampshire Infantry Regiment. By 1880, they had moved to Concord, New Hampshire, and were living in a boarding house.

Over the next 12 years, Laura had six children. By the mid-to-late 1880s, she was part of the Derry Depot. That's not to be mistaken with East Derry, where the upper crust lived. The Derry Depot was down by the train station, a bustling part of town near the First Baptist Church, the laundry, and the shoe factories.

From her home, Mrs. Darling would have been able to hear the Boston & Maine rolling up the track, carrying passengers from Lawrence to Manchester.

Mrs. Darling must have been as industrious as the people around her, for soon she was running a boarding house called Fair View House. One afternoon, a few "Lynnites" (people from Lynn, Massachusetts) came into town and got so rowdy the fracas hit the local news. The story goes that they arrived at midday, had a few drinks, ended up at Fair View House, and stole Mrs. Darling's silk umbrella. She sent a few Derry boys after them. The thieves were pursued to the train station. Stonecutter Moore (that was not his actual first name), who happened to be on the platform, brought the bad behavior to a standstill. It was said his right arm shot out like a piston rod and dealt a stunning blow to one of the offenders. The tussle was over before it began.

While Laura may have owned a fancy umbrella at one time, her life was often difficult. By 1902, she'd moved from operating the Fair View House to stitching shoes in one of the local factories. That same year the newspaper suggested that she was dreaming of going west. She never left New Hampshire, though. In 1903, she divorced James Darling on the grounds of "extreme cruelty." That was the term for abuse. Eventually, she moved back to Concord where she worked in a factory and lived with a fella named Charles Rowe. She died in 1930 at the New Hampshire State Hospital, the local asylum. She was buried that year in Forest Hill Cemetery in Derry, New Hampshire, with her estranged husband and a son, Dustin.

James Arthur Tyler

James Arthur Tyler, Forest Hill Cemetery, Derry, New Hampshire.

Big Batting Fest: Lawrence Boys Found Themselves Up
Against the Real Thing. A. Tyler Star at Bat

So ran the headline in the July 19, 1907, *Derry Enterprise*. James Arthur Tyler would make that kind of headline again and again because he was, quite simply, an ace at baseball.

James, known as Arthur, was born in 1887 to John Tyler and Martha McCannon. John was a shoe factory worker and the family lived in modest accommodation on South Avenue. While the Tylers might not have had much money to boast about, they sure could play ball.

Arthur was the eldest of four brothers, all of whom followed him onto the field to various acclaim. One younger brother, George "Lefty" Tyler, was an excellent pitcher who went on to the major leagues. Lefty was one of three pitchers in rotation for the Miracle Braves in 1914, the year they clinched the pennant against the Philadelphia Athletics. Behind the plate during Lefty's major league years was his brother Fred

(Clancy). The youngest brother, Bill, never went to the major leagues but was a star in local ball.

Arthur stayed around Derry, got married to Daisy Sturdivant in 1910, and went on to have kids. He was working as a real estate agent in the early 1930s and was very well known around town.

On December 2, 1932, he made headlines again, but this time the reason was far sadder.

Local Insurance Agent Takes Own Life with Shotgun
J. Arthur Tyler, Former Baseball Star, Popular Man of Town
Suicide Victim

Arthur drove himself out to the Derry Athletic Association ballfield one night—the same place all the boys had played years ago—and took his own life. He was found in the morning when a worker passed the scene on the way to the office.

Over 300 people attended his funeral at the First Church before he was laid to rest in Forest Hill. Banks of flowers surrounded the casket, ushering this Derry star into the afterlife.

Elsie Gaskin Griffin

Elsie Gaskin Griffin, Forest Hill Cemetery, Derry, New Hampshire.

Elsie Gaskin appears to be a small footnote on this Griffin family stone, but in life, Elsie was the lead in her own story. She was born in 1882 in Portsmouth, New Hampshire, to the Reverend William Gaskin and Alice Washburn. She grew up with two brothers. She started her career as a public schoolteacher, but soon the Derry Town Library was established, and her father was chosen as the first librarian. Six months after he began, he resigned. Elsie took his place and she remained in the position for over thirty years

Elsie was a career woman. She not only worked as librarian for the town library, but she also taught book repair workshops, led seminars, and was at one time president of the New Hampshire Library Association. The *Derry News* always reported on her travels and social life, both were active. She went abroad, but some of the most fun anecdotes are about her driving her car around New England in the 1920s with her girlfriends and throwing card parties at her house, which was just a few doors down from the library.

In the 1930s, Elsie wrote a short story for the book *More New Hampshire Folk Tales,* which was compiled by the New Hampshire Women's Federation. The tale was titled "Those Wicked Frills" and recounted how her grandmother had been in trouble with the church because she had curly hair and wore too many accessories. It was the opinion of the church elders that she was far too worldly, showing off this kind of style. She was admonished and was told that she could keep her curls because she came by them naturally, but she would have to do away with the material possessions. This she did, but she didn't discard them entirely, for her family knew that tucked away in her chest were caps, cuffs, and other dainty things.

Elsie was often bucking the norm for her time and appears to have come by this trait naturally.

Elsie eventually married, but it wasn't until she was 60 years old. Her husband, Everett Griffin, had lost his first wife, Blanche. They lived out their days in Derry and were buried, together, in Forest Hill Cemetery.

- - - - -

I could go on all day with other stories, but I'll stop here and let you get to your research. I hope you also write short biographies like these. Just a reminder that the stone doesn't have to be plastered with Masonic symbols to reveal a fascinating tale.

Eleven

LOCAL HISTORY CHALLENGE

Now it's time for you to go from the cemetery to the archives. But where do you access information on the dead? Just as with symbols, *it depends*. Appendix IV will give you some ideas for places to start. Then do the following and see what you can find.

1) Locate your favorite headstone in the cemetery or look back on one you've already recorded. Identify clues, such as names, dates, symbols, location, etc.

2) Access a family history database such as Ancestry.com or FamilySearch.org and begin. Use the search functions to narrow in on time and place.

3) Collect birth, marriage, divorce, death, and census records for

your research subject. Using these records, create a timeline of this person's life.

4) Connect with a local historical society—or a city or town library—to identify other potential resources. Useful sources might be the historical newspapers, maps, house histories, town reports, town history books, and more.

5) Look closely across all documents for further clues that could send you to new resources.

6) Write up a short biography and consider sharing. Where? Perhaps with a family member, at a historical society, on an online forum, at the local library's genealogy club, or on social media. Think of those people in your life who like random historical anecdotes. Share it with them.

It's important to remember that historical records are dispersed across physical and digital repositories. A database is a wonderful place to begin; however, your research may lead far beyond the online world, into local history rooms, archives, university and state libraries, and much more. Have fun and don't be afraid to ask questions as you go. Local librarians, archivists, and other custodians of records are typically happy to assist you in navigating their collections.

RESEARCH CHECKLIST

People leave information about themselves in a variety of places. See if you can locate your research subject in any of the following.

- [ ] Birth, marriage, divorce, and death records
- [ ] Census records
- [ ] City directories
- [ ] Newspapers and trade publications
- [ ] Deeds
- [ ] Diaries and letters
- [ ] Military records
- [ ] Naturalization and immigration records
- [ ] School records
- [ ] Church Records
- [ ] Local histories and house histories
- [ ] Maps
- [ ] Photograph and postcard collections
- [ ] Probate records
- [ ] Town reports

TIMELINE

As you collect records,
build a timeline for your research subject.

Date	Event

RESEARCH NOTES

BIOGRAPHICAL SKETCH

RESEARCH CHECKLIST

People leave information about themselves in a variety of places. See if you can locate your research subject in any of the following.

- [ ] Birth, marriage, divorce, and death records

- [ ] Census records

- [ ] City directories

- [ ] Newspapers and trade publications

- [ ] Deeds

- [ ] Diaries and letters

- [ ] Military records

- [ ] Naturalization and immigration records

- [ ] School records

- [ ] Church Records

- [ ] Local histories and house histories

- [ ] Maps

- [ ] Photograph and postcard collections

- [ ] Probate records

- [ ] Town reports

TIMELINE

As you collect records,
build a timeline for your research subject.

Date	Event

RESEARCH NOTES

BIOGRAPHICAL SKETCH

Twelve

LOCATING THE DEAD

Occasionally you'll have a situation where locating a burial place of an ancestor (or research subject) is not straightforward. You go to Findagrave.com or Billiongraves.com and they're simply not represented. Don't give up just yet. These databases are incomplete. Essentially, people volunteer to trek into the cemetery, photograph, and transcribe what's there. This leaves plenty of room for missing plots. First, not all cemeteries are systematically recorded. Second, because each entry is based upon a headstone, those interred without a marker will be unaccounted for.

So, where do you look if your person isn't on these databases? Seek out:

Certificate of Death: The best record to show you the interment location of your deceased is a certificate of death. Especially by the early 20th century, these became quite detailed. They can include personal information of the deceased, the informant, the cause of death, the funeral home, and the place of burial. You can request these at the city, town or state level. Just look for the vital record requests at the city/town, county, or state archives, then follow the instructions.

Death Register: Even if your ancestor didn't have a full certificate, their death could have been registered with the city or town (depending on when vital statistics began). This type of record might not give you the exact cemetery, however, it can tell you which town or city your ancestor died in, and if you know the location, you can identify cemeteries or burial grounds that were established in that area at that time.

Obituary: Many obituaries, especially in more recent times, can give up great details. They can include funeral arrangements, calling hours, and burial information. Locate the ancestor's local newspaper to see if an obituary ran.

Funeral Home Records: A more off-the-beaten path approach would be to connect with the funeral home cited in an obituary or death notice, even from long ago. Some funeral homes have been passed from one generation to the next and are still around. Occasionally, they have old files, registers, or archives. If you see a certain funeral home cited in an obituary, you could reach out to see if they have any records of the burial location of your ancestor. Remember that this is not the funeral home's primary mission. Ask politely and remember that you may be out-of-bounds of their usual services.

Transport Permit: If a body was transported from one town to another between death and burial, a transport permit may exist. While this might not be the first record to look for, some towns/cities have retained transport permits.

Interment Record: Many cemeteries and cemetery employees are good record keepers. Even if your ancestor lacks a headstone, their place of interment may have been recorded. After all, cemetery workers hate to start digging and run into a casket. It's far better to have a clear map and be able to dig in an empty plot. Get local to your ancestor's stomping grounds and connect with the purveyor of those records. Is it the cemetery office, the department of public works, the town clerk, the local sexton, the church?

Community Burial Grounds: Don't forget that some folks aren't going to be buried in the town cemetery (by choice or force). Some might be in the churchyard, community cemetery, or segregated burial ground. Getting a good handle on race, religion, and community of your ancestor might lead you to a graveyard that you hadn't previously considered.

LOCATING THE DEAD

If you're having trouble locating the burial place of your research subject, try the following. Refer to Appendix IV for ideas on where to identify these types of records.

____Death certificate

____Death register

____Obituary

____Funeral home records

____Transport permits

____Interment records

____Community burial grounds

Still not having any luck?
It might be time to expand your search to loved ones. Find death certificates, interment records, etc., for the research subject's siblings, parents, spouses. Are they all in the same cemetery?
If so, it might be worth a visit!

Thirteen

GETTING INVOLVED

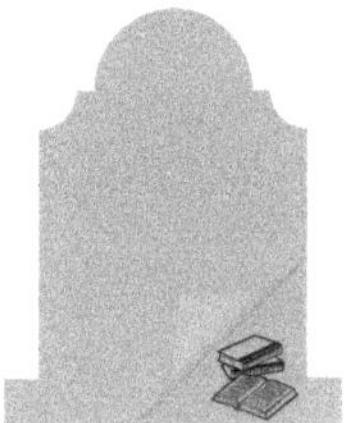

Do you love the cemetery so much you want to get involved? Here are a few ideas to get you started.

1) Run for cemetery commission/trustee. These people are charged with the oversight of the local cemeteries, scheduling maintenance, organizing interments, and sale of grave lots.

2) Join the volunteer organization affiliated with the cemetery. These are often called the "Friends." Many moderate to large cemeteries have "Friends" groups. They support the cemetery in many ways. If you're up for cemetery research and promotion, spring cleanup or planting, this could be a good fit for you.

3) Even if you don't have time for an active "Friends" group, you could volunteer for a one-time cemetery cleanup. In many cases,

all hands on deck is appreciated. This could include everything from picking up flags and twigs to cleaning headstones.

4) Become a Findagrave.com or Billiongraves.com contributor. These are crowdsourced websites where contributors take pictures of headstones and provide transcriptions of them. You can also add genealogical documents or other biographical information. It can be a fun way to contribute to cemetery research.

5) Join the Association of Gravestone Studies. Their mission is to further the study and preservation of gravestones.

6) Get local. What groups in your area are already doing work to support and share the history of the cemetery? Is it the historical society, history museum, heritage commission, public library, or affiliated church? Perhaps you could offer your skills to collaborate and prepare a cemetery tour. I've seen self-guided walking tours, soul strolls, haunted gatherings, role-playing history tours and more. Get creative. Collaborate and build community!

Fourteen

CONCLUSION

The cemetery offers many avenues of discovery. It's a reflection of the local environment, its people, industry, and history. As you walk, you will find clues about days gone by. It's my hope that you gather those clues in the pages of this book, make tracks to the archives, and explore more there. It's my hope that your journey gives you information and a foundation to understanding your local history. Finally, it's my hope that this little cemetery sleuthing adventure leads you down a path of discovery in your own backyard.

Appendix I: Symbols

Anchor: mariner
Angel: heavenly messenger
Bee: a productive life
Bird: flight of the soul
Book: Bible, book of life, scholar, writer, librarian, or teacher
Bull: strength and power
Butterfly: metamorphosis, here or after death
Caduceus: medical worker
Cannon: veteran
Chain links (three): Independent Order of the Oddfellows
Chisel and mallet: craftsman—leather, stone, or wood
Coffin: mortality
Compass and square: Freemasons
Corn: full life, maturity, harvest
Cross: Christianity
Death's-head: mortal remains
Death's-head, winged: mortal remains and ascent of the soul
Dog: guardian, loyalty, and love
Door: embarking on a new journey
Elephant: strength, stature, and wisdom
Engine or gears: engineer
Flame: undying friendship
Flowers (in general): beauty
Handshake: a fond farewell or a warm welcome
Hand with finger pointing up: a soul to heaven

Hand with finger pointing down: God reaching down to bring a
 soul to heaven
Harp: praise
Heart: love
Hoe: farmer
Hourglass: time passing, sands of time
Ivy: friendship, life winding on after death, immortality
Lamb: innocence
Lily or lily of the valley: innocence, purity
Lion: courage, power, honor
Loom: weaver
Maltese cross: firefighter
Mortar and pestle: apothecary or pharmacist
Musical notes or instrument: musician
Musket: veteran
Owl: wisdom
Plow: farmer
Rod of Asclepius: medical worker
Rooster: new dawn in the afterlife, resurrection
Rose: beauty
Rosebud: a life ended before bloom
Scales of justice: judge or lawyer
Shell: eternal life
Snake: eternal life
Soul effigy: mortal remains and ascent of the soul
Star: heavenly realm
Star of David: Jewish
Star, five-pointed: Order of the Eastern Star
Sun: day
Sun rising: renewal or new beginnings
Tree stump: life cut short
Tree: lumberman, woodcrafter, or forester
Urn: mortal remains
Urn, with flame: mortal remains and undying friendship

Urn, with shroud: mortal remains and mourning
Vine: faithfulness, remembrance
Weeping willow: mourning and immortality
Wheel of Buddha: Buddhist
Wheat: farmer or divine harvest
Wreath: everlasting life

Appendix II: Abbreviations

DAR: Daughters of the American Revolution
FATAL: fairest among thousands, altogether lovely
FLT: friendship, love, and truth
FBC: friendship, benevolence, and charity
FOE: Fraternal Order of the Eagles
G: geometry, God
GMG3: Gunner's Mate Petty Officer 3rd Class
GS: Girl Scouts
HA: heavy artillery
HT2: Hull Technician Petty Officer 2nd Class
IOOF: Independent Order of the Oddfellows
K of C: Knights of Columbus
K of P: Knights of Pythias
OES: Order of the Eastern Star
PLEF: purity, love, equality, and fidelity
P of H: Patrons of Husbandry
PS: Pythian Sisters
R: Daughters of Rebekah
RMN3: Radioman (Navigation) Petty Officer 3rd Class
SAR: Sons of the American Revolution
VA: Veterans Affairs

Appendix III: A Grave
Reading List

Gilson, Thomas, and William Gilson. *Carved in Stone: The Artistry of Early New England Gravestones*, Wesleyan University Press, 2012.

Griffith, Michael. *The Speaking Stone: Stories Cemeteries Tell*, University of Cincinnati Press, 2021.

Huey, Lois Miner. *Forgotten Bones: Uncovering a Slave Cemetery*, Millbrook Press, 2016.

Knoblock, Glenn A. *Women of Granite: The Hidden Lives of New Hampshire Women as Seen in the Cemetery, 1674–1992*, published by Arcadia Publishing by arrangement with Fonthill Media LLC, 2021.

Kull, Andrew. *New England Cemeteries: A Collector's Guide*, S. Greene Press, 1975.

Melville, Greg. *Over My Dead Body: Unearthing the Hidden History of Americas Cemeteries*, Harry N. Abrams, 2023.

Neighbors, Joy. *The Family Tree Cemetery Field Guide: How to Find, Record, & Preserve Your Ancestors' Graves*, the Family Tree Books, an imprint of F + W Media, Inc., 2017.

Poole, Robert M. *Section 60: Arlington National Cemetery: Where War Comes Home*, 1st U.S. ed., Bloomsbury, 2014.

——— *On Hallowed Ground: The Story of Arlington National Cemetery*, 1st U.S. ed., Walker & Co., 2009.

Rhoads, Loren. *199 Cemeteries to See Before You Die*, 1st ed., Black Dog & Leventhal Publishers, 2017.

Robinson, David., and Dean R. 1945– Koontz. *Beautiful Death: Art of the Cemetery*, Penguin Studio, 1996.

Rogak, Lisa. *Stones and Bones of New England: A Guide to Unusual, Historic, and Otherwise Notable Cemeteries*, Globe Pequot Press, 2004.

Scee, Trudy Irene. *Garden Cemeteries of New England, 1796–2019*, published by Down East Books, an imprint of Globe Pequot, 2019.

Strangstad, Lynette. *A Graveyard Preservation Primer*, Rowman & Littlefield Publishers; 2nd ed., 2013.

Yalom, Marilyn. *The American Resting Place*, Houghton Mifflin Co., 2008.

Zwicker, Roxie J. *New Hampshire Book of the Dead: Graveyard Legends and Lore*, the History Press, 2012.

Appendix IV: Archives

Cemetery sleuthing done right is a study of individuals, and individuals leave pieces of themselves in a variety of places. Okay, not actual pieces of themselves (though what a find that would be). The point is, historical and genealogical materials are dispersed. There is no one place for extracting information. Each research project has its own path. Databases are a great place to start, but stepping off the standard databases and getting into the local archives will eventually make your research more exciting. Here are a few places to begin.

Paid databases are indicated with a ($) while free databases stand alone.

Foundational Databases

- American Ancestors: https://www.americanancestors.org/ ($) or ask if your local library subscribes.
- Ancestry.com: https://www.ancestry.com ($) or ask if your local library subscribes.
- FamilySearch: https://familysearch.org
- GenealogyBank: https://genealogybank.com ($)
- National Archives and Records Administration (NARA): https://www.archives.gov/

Newspapers

- Advantage Preservation:
  https://directory.advantage-preservation.com
- Chronicling America: https://chroniclingamerica.loc.gov/
- Genealogybank: https://www.genealogybank.com ($)
- Newspapers.com by Ancestry: https://www.newspapers.com/ ($)
- NewspaperArchive: https://newspaperarchive.com/ ($)

Maps

- David Rumsey Historical Map Collection:
  https://www.davidrumsey.com
- Library of Congress (Sanborn Maps Collection):
  https://www.loc.gov/collections/sanborn-maps/
- Norman B. Leventhal Map and Education Center:
  https://www.leventhalmap.org/collections/digital-collections/
- Old Maps Online: https://www.oldmapsonline.org/

Miscellaneous Digital Archives

- Digital Public Library of America: https://dp.la/
- Fulton History: https://fultonhistory.com/
- HathiTrust Digital Library: https://www.hathitrust.org/
- Internet Archive: https://archive.org/
- Library of Congress: https://www.loc.gov/
- World Radio History:
  https://www.worldradiohistory.com/index.htm

Local Digital Archives

Don't skip trying to find out what local digital archives are available. Many archives, libraries, and historical societies work hard to make their collections accessible online. Here are a few examples of wonderful local archives:

- Allen County Public Library Digital Collections: http://contentdm.acpl.lib.in.us/
- Calisphere: https://calisphere.org/
- Digital Commonwealth: https://www.digitalcommonwealth.org/
- Digital Derry Project: https://www.derrypl.org/digital-derry-project
- Indiana Memory: https://indianamemory.contentdm.oclc.org/
- Ohio History Connection: https://www.ohiohistory.org/research/
- Maine Memory Network: https://www.mainememory.net/
- New York Public Library Digital Collections: https://digitalcollections.nypl.org/

Physical Archives

After exhausting your digital resources, it's time to seek out information on foot. Identify physical repositories to continue your research. No idea where to begin? Google will help. So will ArchiveGrid (https://researchworks.oclc.org/archivegrid/). Repositories could be at the town/city, county, or state level. Some reading/research rooms charge a fee while others are free. It's best to call and ask about appointments and holdings prior to making a trip. Get local to your research subject. Think about and identify:

- Town/City/County or State Library
- Town/City/County or State Historical Society

- Town/City/County or State Archives
- Local Experts (librarians, historians, archivists, clerks, records administrators, cemetery workers, etc.)

Appendix V: Bibliography

Books

Atkeson, Thomas Clark. *Semi-Centennial History of the Patrons of Husbandry*, Orange Judd Company, 1916.

Boy Scouts of America. *Boy Scouts of America: The Official Handbook for Boys*, The Boy Scouts of America, 1911.

Carmack, Sharon DeBartolo. *Your Guide to Cemetery Research*, Betterway Books, 2002.

Girl Scouts of the United States of America. *Scouting for Girls: Official Handbook of the Girl Scouts*, The Girl Scouts, Inc., 1920.

Gore, Mrs. Moody P. and Speare, Mrs. Guy E. *More New Hampshire Folk Tales*, Mrs. Guy E. Speare, 1936, p. 158.

Grosh, A. B. *The Odd-Fellow's Improved Manual: Containing the History, Defence, Principles, and Government of the Order; The Instructions of Each Degree, and Duties of Every Station and Office in Odd-Fellowship; with Directions and Forms for Laying Corner-Stones, Dedicating Cemeteries, Halls, Etc., Marshalling Processions, Etc,; Also, Odes, with Music for Various Occasions, and The Most Needed Business Forms*, Theodore Bliss & Co., 1871.

How, Jeremiah. *The Freemason's Manual, or, Illustrations of Masonry: Containing, in Addition the Rites Sanctioned by the United Grand Lodge and the Grand Chapter of England and Wales, the Mark Man and Mark Master, A Full Account of All the Degrees Included in the Ancient and Accepted Rite, Together with the Knights Templar Degree, Red Cross of Rome and Constantine, The Royal Order of Scotland, and Brief Notice of the Rites Professions to Be Connected with Freemasonry Etc., Etc.,* John Hogg, 1881.

Keister, Douglas. *Stories in Stone: A Field Guide to Cemetery Symbolism and Iconography,* Gibbs Smith, Publisher, 2004.

Liungman, Carl G. *Dictionary of Symbols* ABC-CLIO, 1991.

Mackey, Albert Gallatin. *An Encyclopedia of Freemasonry and Its Kindred Sciences Comprising the Whole Range of Arts, Sciences and Literature as Connected with the Institution* (Vol. 1), Moss & Co., 1878.

Mackey, Albert Gallatin, *An Encyclopedia of Freemasonry and Its Kindred Sciences Comprising the Whole Range of Arts, Sciences and Literature as Connected with the Institution* (Vol. 2), Moss & Co., 1878.

Macoy, Robert. *Ritual of the Order of the Eastern Star. A Book of Instruction for the Organization, Government and Ceremonies of Chapters of the Order in Every Department,* Robert Macoy Publisher, 1876.

Stevens, Albert Clark. *The Cyclopaedia of Fraternities; A Compilation of Existing Authentic Information and the Results of Original Investigation as to the Origin, Derivation, Founders, Development, Aims, Emblems, Character, And Personnel of More Than Six Hundred Secret Societies in the United States,* Hamilton Printing and Publishing Company, 1899.

Van Valkenburg, John. *The Knights of Pythias Complete Manual and Text-Book, Containing, the History, Defence, Principles, and Government of the Order,* Moss and Company, 1877.

Articles

Benes, Peter. "John Wight, the Hieroglyph Carver of Londonderry." *Old-time New England* vol. 64, no. 2 (Oct.-Dec. 1973), pp. 31-41.

"Deaths: Mrs. Elsie Griffin," *The Derry News* (Derry, New Hampshire) 19 April 1956. p. 3, c. 5.

"Derry Doings," *The Derry News* (Derry, New Hampshire) 10 January 1902, p. 1, c. 6.

"Local Insurance Agent Takes Own Life with Shotgun," *The Derry News* (Derry, New Hampshire) 2 December 1932, p. 8, c. 3 and 4.

Lowenthal, William. "'Suitable Grave Stones': The Workshop of Moses Davis of Nashua (Nashville), New Hampshire." *Markers* XXIII (2006), pp. 36-71.

"Order of the Pythian Sisterhood," *Portland Sunday Telegram* (Portland, Maine) 3 September 1905, p. 16.

Prakash, M. and J. Carlton Johnny. "Things you don't learn in medical school: Caduceus." *Journal of Pharmacy & Bioallied Sciences* vol. 7, Suppl 1 (2015): S49-50. doi:10.4103/0975-7406.155794

"Rhowdyism," *The Derry News* (Derry, New Hampshire) 31 October 1890, p. 1, c. 3.

Watters, David H. "'Fencing ye Tables': Scotch-Irish Ethnicity and the Gravestones of John Wight." *Markers* XVI (1999), pp. 174-209.

Websites:

Association for Gravestone Studies:
https://www.gravestonestudies.org/

Boy Scouts of America: https://www.scouting.org/

Davis Funeral Home: https://www.davisfuneralhomenh.com

Daughters of the American Revolution: https://www.dar.org/

Department of Veterans Affairs: https://www.va.gov/

Fraternal Order of the Eagles: https://www.foe.com/

Girl Scouts of the USA: https://www.girlscouts.org/

Knights of Columbus: https://www.kofc.org/

Knights of Pythias: https://www.pythias.org/

National Cemetery Administration: https://www.cem.va.gov/

National Grange: https://www.nationalgrange.org/

Oddfellows Sovereign Grand Lodge: https://odd-fellows.org/

Order of the Eastern Star: https://easternstar.org/

Order of the Pythian Sisters: https://pythiansisters.org/

Rebekahs: https://odd-fellows.org/about/rebekahs/

Sons of the American Revolution: https://www.sar.org/

NOTES

NOTES

NOTES

NOTES

SKETCHES

SKETCHES

SKETCHES

SKETCHES